House of Dreams

Thérèse Corfiatis

House of Dreams
Selected Poems

For Paul, Yousif, Kye, Jason, Eddie and Lucy

House of Dreams: Selected Poems
ISBN 978 1 76041 203 6
Copyright © text Thérèse Corfiatis 2016
Cover photo © janonkas

First published in this form 2016 by
GINNINDERRA PRESS
PO Box 3461 Port Adelaide 5015 Australia
www.ginninderrapress.com.au

Contents

Cameron Street Cameo	7
A Memory of Eastern European Migration	11
Behind the Screen	13
Ferihegy Airport	14
Four Candles For a Magyar	16
Welcome Home	19
Stone	21
Gulls and Sky	23
Morning Walk	24
Sea Horse	25
The Seventh Image	26
Agapanthus In Moonlight	28
A Memory of Goolwa Beach	29
Figures of Eight	30
Blue-winged Angels	31
House of Dreams	32
Choir Practice	34
Helsinki	35
Ice Age Oracle	39
Lamentation On a Tribal Beach	42
Transit of Venus – Alien Encounter	44
The Ballad of Johnny	46
Death in Whyalla	48
Immigrants	49
Patterns of Winter	52
News Item from Baghdad	53
Russell Square	55
Sanitised Terms of Warfare	56
Howard and Rudd Symphony	57
Variations on Clouds	59

Walking and Watching	61
Wedge-tailed Eagle	62
Acropolis at Night	63
Patmos	64
And So They Wait for Love	66
Sky Elephants	68
Sparrowsurge	69
Chapel Road	70
Dawn Drifter	71
Magnolias	72
Sunday Morning Rural Portrait	73
Wind, Roses and Wrens	74
Tree Ship	75
Winter's Stage	76
Armies of Light	77
Tell Me	79
Acknowledgements	81

Cameron Street Cameo

South Hobart

First memories are of peering
Through the garden gate,
Wooden palings with gaps between them,
Staring out curiously upon the world.

Above me
Gigantic high-domed sky.
It was then I loved the colour blue.

A red brick church
Soared to the right of me,
In my mind a monumental structure –
And my mother's garden
Bordered with small neat stones.

The old house seemed so huge,
Narrow staircases ascending
To attic rooms at either end.
I played there with make-believe friends
As real to me as my own voice.

I awoke one night
(Or was I dreaming?)
Stretching up to look out
Over the window sill,
And from my upstairs room
I thought I saw a small pink elephant.

One day my plaits got caught
Tangling in the washer's wringer
Hair starting to tear from the scalp.
Shrieks of help sent mother rushing in.
Just in time she saved me.

And a memory
Of waiting for my father to come home.
He walked briskly from the bus stop
Up Angelsea St.
His long coat flapping in the wind,
His cigarette trailing little clouds of smoke.
I would run to meet him and
He would stop and stand quite still,
A concerned look upon his face,
Catching me up in strong arms.

My little brothers,
One still a baby, with flaxen curls
Dimpled cheeks and cupid lips
Looked like a pretty doll.
The older one, dark-eyed, gentle, silent –
Always holding back
As if the world was too dangerous.
I looked out for him.

Sundays were church days.
Hard pews smelt of polished wood.
The priest's silken voice
Made it difficult to stay awake.
The beautiful statue of the Madonna,
Her poor son nailed in agony upon a cross,
Head drooping to one shoulder, eyes closed.
I felt sorry for Mary.

Rows of tapered candles glowed softly
Altar flowers brilliant
Lighting up the space around them,
My grandparent's loving smiles.

I tell myself
What value are these memories
To anyone else?

Yet, I am compelled to write them,
For in writing them they will not die.
These tiny inconsequential things
Can leave their stamp
Upon the page,
Like the small neat stones
Bordering my mother's garden,
Or my father's long coat
Flapping in the wind.

The old house is gone now,
Demolished,
But the church remains.
We children were baptised there.
The red bricks
Glisten in the sun like fire,
As if harbouring the knowledge
Of a family's trials.

A Memory of Eastern European Migration

Post-World War II Hungary

How do people
Bear the loss of everything
In a single day?

Where do they go
The homeless ones
Drifting
Between dispossession and despair?
The body's senses shut down,
Cold, hunger, shock denied.

Survival is one foot placed before the other.

This tide of human flotsam
Creates its own sea,
Voyaging the endless road
Upon thin worn-out shoes.
Crescendos of pain and melancholia
Sow seeds of grief along the way.
This is the cruellest harvest,
A parting from their native soil
Not of their choosing.

Ghosts of ancient forefathers,
Parthians, Huns, Avars, Tartars
Keen upon a haunted wind.
Cathedrals of blood and bone
Steer a course,
But in what direction?
There is no turning back.

Patriotism immolates
In the flames of human carnage.
Acrid smoke stings the eyes.
No. These are not tears they weep.
There are no tears left.

How heavy the price?
How long the memory?

Behind the Screen

The broken man
through decades of his broken life
hunted shadows of an elusive dream.
He contemplates his world of sorrow
from behind the screen.

In that place of veiled illusions
fragmented thought beats vainly on the air,
the oracles inside his head are laughing,
for who is there to know or care?

Oh, how he longs for night
yes, prays for it,
sleep releases him from pain,
where joyful childhood memories
can breathe and walk and live again.

There, in the centre of his heart
high mountains soar
and shift the balance for a moment
to uplift his soul.
Alas, this is a fleeting thing
and cannot make him whole.

Dawn awakens him
to herald yet another lonely day,
in which he contemplates his world of sorrow
from behind the screen,
A broken man who lives a broken dream.

Ferihegy Airport

Budapest

Before the plane touched down

before the onboard Magyars
started whooping for joy
as the wheels bounced along the tarmac

a thought flashed to mind
of a painting in my childhood home

wild horses galloping across a flat plain
cushioned between earth and sky

and I understood what freedom meant
this symbolic running of the horses
manes and tails swept behind them
in glorious streaming banners

and as we flew in
I marvelled at the flatness of the land
at the noisy shouts and whistles
of those rowdy Magyars
filling the plane's belly with their whooping
unashamedly patriotic
riding the plane's structure
just as cowboys of the Puszta ride their horses
reckless, unafraid, sure of themselves
part of the land that fashioned them

This was my first connection
to the place of my ancestors
as I flew through the sky
held between heaven and earth

every breath to become a voyage of discovery

Four Candles For a Magyar

In memory of Attila Ferenc Ágoston, born Budapest, Hungary, 1/12/1925, died Penguin, Tasmania, 4/09/2006

The church exudes a Scandinavian simplicity
Reinforced by the stark coffin
On its bier,
Its only ornament a crucifix
And my father's homeland flag.

The priest, my brother and I
Make three,
The fourth presence here
Immortality.

Hushed silence is broken
By the thrumming sea.
Its funereal dirge unsettles me.

Strangely, when I close my eyes
I imagine Vikings, wielding axes
Chopping down the vaulted door.

I am everywhere and nowhere,
Spilling over the entire earth,
My father's ancestry
Clutching at the here and now.

His truths and falsehoods still burn,
A fever raging, shaping my emotion.
I sit, half-mad
The weight of all his centuries
Crushing my bones.

Geography shifts –
The drumming of horse's hooves,
Warriors, battles, displacement and despair,
The rumbling of tank wheels –
My sanity stretched, trampled
Exploding outwards
Into the golden cross of Christendom,
So that in my sorrow
I am consumed by this Hungarian
Who spoke of blood and church and country
And died with this belief.

This pivotal moment of my life
Enters me, like the point of a sword
Turning sharply inwards.
Genetic fragments of memory cut into my veins.

One half of me is gone,
My father's last words
Written on life's page,
Yet, I remain, unsure
Dry-eyed,
Blinking in the stain-glassed streams
Of dappled weeping light,
A nervous actor debuting on a new stage.

Here, in this little seaside church
We pray at the altar,
Sincere entreaties spoken
For a soul to find peace.

Three times the priest
Circles the coffin.

He sings to the saints and angelic hosts –
A chant of Latin homage released
In perfectly formed vowelled jewels
For my father's spirit to be lifted up.

Sprinkled holy water
Bounces off the coffin like diamonds.
Incense burner swings sickly sweet.

Four candles burn.
One for my brother and I.
Two for our rebirth of hope.

It is over.

Welcome Home

My childhood home is empty now.
It stands at the bottom of the hill
Like a forlorn sentinel.
Ghosts of the past
Reluctantly leave.

I feel unsettled
As I run my fingers
Over the old books,
Especially the ones
Belonging to my father.

I read the words phonetically,
Hungarian pronounced exactly as written,
But the language frustrates
And is a beautiful enigma.

I remember as a child
Being enchanted at its sound,
The way the words were spoken
Like a long epic poem,
The peculiar intonation of the first syllable
Rising softly, then falling
In a succession of rippling vowels.

The house is not unfriendly,
But the rooms
Hold a faint trace
Of pain and abandonment.

It is a house of broken dreams.

The dreams cling in fragments
To windows, timberwork
Rusty roof and chimney bricks
And cry out to be free.
'Let us live!' they cry
'We have been confined for so long.
Do not be afraid to touch us.
We are real.'

In the front passage
Someone stares back at me
From the hallstand mirror.

She is the daughter of a survivor
Born after the nightmare
That was World War II.
It's a miracle she's here.

I reach out to touch her cheek
And welcome her home.
I understand where she comes from.
I know her face.

It belongs to me.

Stone

In my dream
There is always this landscape of wildness.
Rugged peaks, valleys, hills –
Massive boulders
Sculpting the space around them,
Stone and earth descending
Into heaving, restless seas.

Immense clawed waves
Relentlessly scrape sheer escarpments
With white frenzied fingers.

And always
The sound of water wearing stone,
As if a thousand centuries
Are but a moment,
Unaware of its intrusion.

High, high up
Much higher than the torn and broken cliffs
A pale blue sky thinly oscillates.
I inhabit those frozen spheres
Weightless and free.

Far below
Rust-brown craggy outcrops
Guard a moss-covered gateway
Primeval and forsaken.

The stones sing of glassy ice,
Soft summer sun, wildflowers
Bare skin and circles of fire.

Alone in this wilderness
But at one in the centre of all things
Known to me,
My face is the face of another,
Carved in stone, frozen in time.

The dream brings me home.

Gulls and Sky

So calm and bright this blue-green sea.

High above
Great columns of white cloud rise
Greek temples suspended upon air.
In those hovering dominions, gulls
Drift upon sea winds
Gliding into cloud, re-
Appearing into solid bluest sky.
They soar in a procession of outstretched wings,
Worshipping water, wind and light
Crying out in homage
To the altar of their sky.

Morning Walk

A ruffled band of feathered amputees
one-legged gulls balance by the sea's edge
surveying watery-grey kingdoms.

Stillness pervades all
but there is an overlaying hint of heaviness,
an eerie light emanating
from within dark billowing clouds,
as if something waits
and shall announce
'Behold,
I am the Light of the World.'

Sea Horse

Winged arms
Propel this miniature Pegasus
Through sunlit water.

Tiny arching head
Curves into a tessellated spine
Ending in an S-shaped tail.

The little amber horse
Is a living treble clef,
Pitching forward
Into the trembling
Lines and spaces
Of the ocean's great song.

The Seventh Image

Little Bird, Dream Stealer

I have gone out of myself in sleep.
Restless dreams propel me
through a canopy of shifting darkness.

I am sinking
drifting downwards,
searching for a glimmer of communion.

Somewhere a bird's cry
pierces the layers
binding heaven and earth.

Fluttering to my shoulders
its beating wings
cool the air upon my cheek.

Little bird, where is my home?
Your bright eyes reflect a truth
I cannot find when I awake.

And then, through your eyes
I glimpse a journeying people.
Smiling, they beckon me to follow.

Like a sighing wind they travel
forests of beech and dappled larch,
voices rippling like a stream.

Sometimes they walk flat, treeless plains
singing songs I have heard before
in words I do not understand.

I run to join them
but heavy legs defeat me.
Blinded by tears, my way is lost.

Little bird, why do you steal my dreams
and scatter them like feathers
before an endless sweeping sky?

Agapanthus In Moonlight

Moonlit agapanthus cluster
Broad fleshy leaves
Giant starfish swimming on a midnight sea
Tapered stems pierce shadows
Pointing skywards
Singular in purpose –
Soft purplish flowers
Burst out in sprays of miniature constellations
Heads nodding in obeisance to the stars

A Memory of Goolwa Beach

(South Australia)

For Joseph

We had gone to explore
the storm-tossed beach,
wind howling in our ears.
The ocean raged and crashed,
thundering to the shore.

You were chasing gulls and charging
through thick banks of drifting foam,
when suddenly your elfin face
looked back for me – unsure
as if the world and all its power
was too much for you to bear.

I came and held you close
within the circle of my arms,
my little one, so tiny
needing comfort from his fear.

How cherished the memories
our hearts recall,
never the huge moment,
only the small.

Figures of Eight

We drove down from Airey's Inlet
to find a picnic spot beneath tall gums
a small, green pond
cress-covered water
lily-pads and stalks rising up like little sentinels
emerald reeds quivering in a creamy fringe.

A T-shaped wooden walkway
looked happy to meet us,
absorbing our footsteps
as we fed the ducks leftover bread.

This miniature wetland displayed its diversity.
Purple swamp hens, marsh hens
ducks, frogs and tiny fish
waders, seabirds, insects
but best of all –
two brown eels spiralling in graceful figures of eight,
snake-like heads, little mouths open
come to inspect the feeding frenzy.

Curious, camouflaged in deeper murky water,
they wrote their underwater hieroglyphics
amazing us with their sinuous coiling,
leaving cryptic messages
of waterborne voyages beneath our feet.

Blue-winged Angels

Summer drapes herself
About the sky,
The splash of blue-winged angels everywhere,
Clouds have fled in awe
For such magnificence
Cannot be defied
To blot or leave a single wisp of white
Against the azure wash of God's own eye.

Blue harbours memories
Of perfect summer light
Flooding through the windows
Of my childhood room,
Anticipation of roaming bushland
(Such carefree, balmy days)
A time when I was truly free,
And even now in middle-age
A part of it still stirs in me.

And so, these happy thoughts return
On this perfect summer day,
As I watch the blue-winged angels
Drape themselves about the sky,
And feel the pleasure of this moment –
For they have taught me how to fly.

House of Dreams

In my dream
the little house
is set down by the sea.

Sweeping arc of beach
joins it to an isthmus
long and thin.

Ancient hills
surround the house
in layered rings of sloping green,
quiet solitude and isolation,
I cannot see a living thing.

Small windows
panes like eyes
moss-covered roof,
white-washed stone.

Inside its walls
a person waits –
I do not know them yet
but they know me.

How can I journey
to this place
to meet a person
I do not know?

Will its occupant
divine my questions,
answer them
and set me free?

Both exist
so clear and vivid
in my little house of dreams.

Choir Practice

Colossal clouds build up
cathedrals
levitating in the sky

Against horizons
softer clouds
congregate like monks
chanting in a circle
a crescendo building
heaven's vaults echoing
voices on the wind.

Helsinki

Helsinki bristles and bustles with self-awareness.

Freed from a long history of occupation
Where East and West
Shackled her with war, terror and hunger,
Finns brim with patriotic pride
Reinforced by a mother tongue
Once despised, forbidden
But now revered.

City's architecture diverse;
Senaatintori Square, white and pristine
Neo-classical.
From its sweeping granite steps
A beautiful harbour spreads out
Like a turquoise fan
Dotted with islands and skerries.

Cobblestoned streets
Burst with inner-city buildings
Leaning shoulder to shoulder.
Compact Nordic simplicity,
Multi-storeyed in quaint yellows
Russet-reds, tangerines, blues.
Decorative wrought-iron balconies
Splash colour with bright summer flowers.

Market Square is crammed with shoppers
Buying every kind of produce
In every Baltic language –
Lithuanian, Estonian, Polish, Latvian
Russian, Swedish –
Unfamiliar yet enthralling.

On the crest of a hill
Uspenski Cathedral,
Largest Russian Orthodox Church
In Western Europe,
Its star-encrusted cupola, brilliant painted icons
A feast for the eyes,
Colour, space and light flooding in
Preparing the way for the second coming
With splendid visions for true believers.

A few streets away
Temppeliaukio,
A stunning modern church,
Below ground, built into solid rock
Capped with a clear glass and copper dome
So that at night
It glows strangely
Like a UFO softly hovering.

The mind is stretched and challenged
With visual overload,
New perceptions.

The railway station flanked by
Giant granite guards,
Instantly recognisable to travellers.
Green-laced trees line wide avenues
Arcing into shade and shelter.
Strong smell of coffee
From al fresco diners.

Famous blue glass in Aleksanterinkatu
Prized and precious,
Draws tourists to shop windows.
City parks are full of workers
Basking in the lunchtime sun.

The city is cosmopolitan, modern
Wealthy and comfortable –
One solitary beggar by a hotel door.

Everything is mellowed and softened
By Scandinavian light.
Sky and sea are heightened by it.

At day's end
Dusk hovers in violet veils
So that boulders and rocks
Shimmer like gem stones
Crafted from pure glass
Adrift on mauve waters.

Trees shimmer,
Trunks encased in pale gold.
Ancient spirits of forest, water and wind
Breathe softly,
Commuters oblivious to their presence.

Ice Age Oracle

Inside the cave
the girl dreamed strange things
and woke unsettled.

Beyond the cave
a bleak frozen vista,
hunters returning, wrapped in furs
ice-covered beards and brows,
words mumbled from shivering lips
a perilous undertaking
with little to show for all their effort.

The people gnawed dried flesh of animals
to fend off hunger and cold.

Darkness continued
no ball of fire in the sky,
until one morning
its golden disc, half rising
shed feeble light across the land.

Water bags, spears, possessions
gathered into bundles,
feet bound in hides
they walked out into the light
following the sun's rays,
and when its golden disc
sank below the line of earth and sky
huddled close for warmth and comfort
chanting songs of life and food and shelter.

The girl dreamed once more
of an entity, multi-limbed
rising straight and tall
its body fused into the ground,
one of an army of such beings upon the earth.

'Tomorrow,' it said,
'tomorrow you will find me.
I will show you the way.'

She told her people.

They ridiculed and scolded.
Eyes averted
she walked behind them.

They travelled many days and nights,
the ball of fire stronger, warmer –
descending from mountains and high valleys
to a place no longer frozen –
waters flowed
earth shimmered in spiked green fur.

It was here their footsteps stopped
and in that silence
the girl looked up,
the tribe parting like a knife on flesh
to give her way.

She walked forward
whispering 'Tomorrow',
and stood before the great tree,
her vision fulfilled.

In veneration
blood-kin touched her face and body
trying to absorb her power,
a wreath of leaves set upon her head,
new skin for a drum
placed reverently into her hands,
her calling acknowledged.

They named her 'Dream Speaker'
and journeyed on
into new awakenings.

Lamentation On a Tribal Beach

Northern Tasmania

Day dims
As the world slips away.
A sky, trembling and pale
Shifts in a kaleidoscope of darkening grey.

Ocean flails wet, cold stones
Of a desolate shore,
Beach resembling a broken spine –
Twisted bands of kelp
Lay stretched and writhing
Contorted into painful shapes,
Moving like muscle and bone.

The startled wide eye of a white moon
Spreads frail light.
Wind groans and keens –
A thing that lives,
A hurt, open mouth
Somersaulting grief through the air
A sarcophagus of lamentation
Spilling everywhere.

I thought I was alone
In this deserted place.
Out of nowhere
Shadows emerge,
Dark figures glide and flit
Upon the sandy shore.
I hear them calling
As I turn to see
White sails of ghostly wooden ships
Carrying their children away.

Transit of Venus – Alien Encounter

Transit of Venus occurred 8/6/2004

The Transit of Venus began everything,
Leading Captain Cook to our shores,
Paradise transformed; a dumping ground
For felons and unfortunate whores.
So started the birth of our nation
Tolling the bell of annihilation
For Aboriginal degradation.

Here in this marvellous Great Southern Land
We have built new prisons upon desert sand,
Boat-people, but of a different race,
Refugees who sew the lips on their face
In a quest for freedom some never attain,
Done nevertheless, in freedom's name.

We've forgotten to consult in matters divine,
Glued to our TV sets, sipping wine,
Fed a diet of Bush's abominable speech,
Watching Iraqis led out like dogs on a leash.
Oh, how they relish American peace.

The Middle East is a place that sounds so far away,
Yet we hear of its horrors at home every day,
Sharon, the mad despot, bombs his brothers to hell
And tortures his citizens for the truths that they tell.
Hamas fights for a country stolen and shattered,
But when has Palestine ever mattered?

The old order is dying, Reagan lays cold,
The ex-movie star is beginning to mould,
Howard palavers on Dunkirk's dead shore,
Where heads of great nations glorify war,
They forget what men died for,
Was is some sort of game?
A way to depopulate in democracy's name?

Heavenly signs and wonders, as brief as they are
Mean nothing to them, they don't gaze at stars,
And here beneath our Antipodean sky
Reconciliation is still a dirty white lie.

The Transit of Venus has passed overhead,
While on earth we continue to bury our dead,
Hallelujah, hallelujah, let the chorus ring loud,
A new age is dawning, world leaders are proud,
Their achievements are many, their deeds are so wise,
But where is the light that once shone in their eyes?

The Ballad of Johnny

A memory of Prime Minister John Howard

Johnny's not sorry.
He made a pretence of regret
But it isn't over yet.

We know he didn't poison waterholes
Or snatch babies
From their mother's arms.
We know he never massacred a tribe
Or orchestrated a diatribe,
But we know his father knew
And his father before him
That sheep and cattle
Were counted on a census,
But never a black man, black woman or black child.
Not till nineteen sixty-seven
Did a black man count in white man's heaven.

Johnny has his own special dreaming,
A head crammed full of clever scheming.
Iron ore and rich uranium
Crushed with the bones of a black man's cranium.

What's wrong with the leader of our nation?
He's guilty by association.
He says he can't forgive
But he can forget.
Johnny, Johnny, it's not over yet.

Johnny, Johnny, come out to play,
Let's watch black kids sniff their lives away,
Johnny, Johnny, your legacy,
Is death, disease and poverty.

Speak for yourself.
Don't dare speak for me.

Death in Whyalla

For Guy Ravanelli

He told me of Sahara's nights,
The great cathedrals of silence,
The vast heavens
That stunned him with their beauty.
It was there
That he existed on another plane.

History could not wait for him,
It marched relentlessly
Expelling his family from Algeria
To a homeland unknown for generations,
And like the Bedouin
Restless for new horizons
He led them far from France
To Australia's distant shore.

Sons and daughters wed,
Raising families of their own,
His sweet wife taken suddenly
Making him a partner to grief,
Love lost too soon.

It seemed appropriate that he died
With summer waning
On the desert's fringe.
Desert places and their histories
Ran in his veins like sand,
And so, the desert took him back
Even though it was a foreign land.

Immigrants

A drifting boat upon the Tigris
Carried you
Through a childhood of golden heat and honey –
Gilded days
Canaries singing in their cage.

Smells of oranges and jasmine,
Musk and spices
Milling all about you,
Rose syrup on your fingertips,
Rolling in your mouth,
The taste all gone now, washed away.

And on those burning summer nights
An ecstasy of dazzling stars,
Perfumed petals softly falling
Showering graces on your head,
Your adolescence covered by the raven hair
And red lips of smooth women –
A land bequeathed to men and might and semen.

Adrift now upon sleepless nights
You crave for poppies
To numb your grieving,
Alienated in a land of gum and wattle
Where winter days are damp and cold.

I watch your profile,
Hawk-like, searching out the shadows,
Hunting down confusion,
Misplaced, like a half-forgotten smile,
Worn out and resigned,
Beaten down by your misplacement,
Always the brooding foreigner,
Your juices frozen over with regret
And silent longing.

How could you know I understand?
I see the memories haunt and cloud your eyes.

Belonging cannot blossom in a land
Where tongues are harsh and brutal
And voices sing in a straight line
Flat and joyless, like its people.
We grieve for what we cannot have.

Misplaced by birth, we are always
Moving between two spheres,
A blur out of mind's reach,
Our feet placed on each side of the river,
The mismatched offspring of foolish parents,
Forgotten bloodlines,
No central fusion of nourishing roots,
Our tree weakened by the cracking earth,
The well run dry.

Your eyes lock into mine.

We laugh together in unspoken understanding
And wish blessings on our children.

Patterns of Winter

This winter night
In bright moonlight
Mottled clouds cluster way up high
Like a pond of swimming trout
Sleek and sinuous.

Twinkling stars
Glitter like little eyes,
Wispen clouds drift as silver tails flick
Swimming gracefully across the heavens.

The speckled sea below
Is a sheening inversion of the sky,
A giant chalice patterned and formed
In filigreed swirlings.

In the breathing vaults of atmosphere
Icy vapours rise and fall,
Prayers from the lips of winter
Softly whispered upon the breasting night
Overlaying everything with wonder.

News Item from Baghdad

It's summer
in one of the hottest cities on earth,
news footage shows women shaking hoses
to catch last precious drops –
buckets half empty
like drawing water from stone.
Unbearably cruel conditions
no infrastructure rebuilt
despite promises sworn.

How has this happened
in the land of two rivers
this destruction and carnage
this theft of resources
slow death of a people?

Iraq gave the world its first farmers
irrigation systems,
encoded humanity's first laws
invented the wheel and brewing of beer
used astronomy and astrology
fusing them into the fabric of daily life
and built a tower to heaven
desiring to placate nature and the gods.

They wrote annals on medicine,
possessed doctors who understood
how someone can die of a broken heart,
revered poets and musicians
adored flowers and fine clothing,
distilled perfumes,
crafted intricate works of art,
built modern cities to equal any today.
We owe them so much for all that we know.

Its summer
in one of the hottest cities of earth.
Let them drink sand.

Russell Square

London

I saw the carnage
At King's Cross Station,
The double-decker bus
Blown apart at Russell Square.

It linked me to a memory
Of a wounded Iraqi freedom fighter
Propped against a mosque wall
Grimacing with pain, half-dead
His arm raised in surrender.

A bullet exploded
From an American gun.
Nowhere to hide
Nowhere to run.

Dying for a freedom is an individual thing,
But dying for a cause
Harbours terror without end.

Sanitised Terms of Warfare

'Enemy combatants'
are in truth
freedom fighters
struggling against occupation.

'Co-lateral damage'
are words that excuse
countless murdered civilians
disappeared, like the dark side of the moon.

'Rendered'
is to give in return,
but in the war on terror
it means unlawful detainment,
torture and death without trial.

The art of war from millennia past
makes more sense
than the misery modern humans inflict.

Macedonians drove nails
into the heels of the dead
to prevent their spirits from returning.

In the 21st century
Facebook and Internet
become pathways for revenants.

Howard and Rudd Symphony

A work in progress

Mortal beings that we are
Life is a circus.
Eat bread, watch football.
Go to work, pay the rent.
Copulate, read the newspaper.
Hang the washing.

Bits of ourselves left out to dry.

All hail the hundred-dollar bill.
Things are important,
Not people.

In the last rays of the setting sun
Ocean glints like diamonds
(Reinforcing the 'money' theme)
And fishes swim
Oblivious to our world of chaos.

We are trapped in water.
Our bodies swim in it.
Blood, tears, sweat, secretions
Movements of the lower bowel.
We swim in food and drink
And shit.
Well, just a little bit.

We are dying in stages,
Rock of ages,
Sand in the crack of our bums.
The mind numbs.
Common sense evacuates the brain
Like the contents of our lower bowel.

Desecration of our nation.
Laws upon laws upon laws.
We can lock up people,
Hold them against their will
Especially if they worship in a mosque
Or visit each other late at night
In foreign garb.

Beware the enemy within.
Shades of Stalin creeping in.

Democracy has died.
The country has gone to the dogs
Yet dogs make more sense
Than the barking voices of parliament.
Our nation is shamed.
Global humiliation.

Death and taxes are our only certainty.
But what about the coffin nails
If there are no trees for wood
Or water to grow them?

Variations on Clouds

Spring Trees, Crescent Moon and Cloud

Crescent moon hooks to trailing cloud
flashes of gold, as wind scuds over sky
like an earring uncovered by streaming hair.
Spring trees resemble spun fairy floss
glittering beneath streetlights –
blossoms swirl like confetti on the wind,
sugary treats for the eye's indulgence.

Swimming Sky Whale and Cloud

Solid expanse of dark-grey sky
hints of blue seeping through
transforming heaven into stippled cloud –
Ah, there it is! A whale's back lifting
riding into cloud
huge, forever swimming.

Gum Tree Music and Clouds

Wind sings high in the gums
soughing troughs of green
are swaying choirs of branches
leaves and tree tops –
energy pulsing upwards
merging into moving cloud.

Cloud Soup

Luxury in solitary moments –
early morning birdsong, crisp winter air
lawn tips like frosted icing
a huge green cake
ready for the slicing,
bird restaurant open all hours
beaks at the ready.
Thin cloud streaks horizon –
vermicelli strands
promise a good soup of the day.

Walking and Watching

Into the landscape
I am walking and watching.

Spring winds bluster in,
sea churns blue-white,
ragged tatters
lift up from bright horizons
trying to fly away.

My body feels disconnected
a thin shell without substance
as if all the frenzied movement and light
have made physicality inconsequential.

I observe the panorama
or is the universe
observing me, observing it?

Are we aware of each other?

Nothing else matters
but the walking and watching.

Wedge-tailed Eagle

You roll out the wind
In a majestic fanfare
Trailing joy in the high halls of heaven.

Your soaring and spiralling
An orchestra of movement
Weaving beautiful songs on the air.

With effortless flight
Your wings bequeath words
Pure poetry inscribed in the sky.

Eagle
You are everything that speaks to freedom.
Give me just one of your days.

Acropolis at Night

Athens

Upon its high place, Acropolis at night
sentinel of Athens,
radiant in amber-saffron light
ethereal, rising up like a vision
columns majestic
like bones of a skeleton, housing
body and soul of a nation

otherworldly
an aura clings to its marble
prayers and offerings ascend
as if the dream-life of gods and people
are fused into the balmy air
breathing out sweet hope
for all mankind

Patmos

Dodecanese Islands

Looking down and out
from a high place
the predominant colour is pale gold,
rock and sand-strewn beaches
air and light
humming with a sense of expectation
not felt on any other Greek island.

Devoid of trees for the most
an occasional grotto,
but rock and stone abundant
the island from this high viewing point
shaped a little like a Hydra
bulbous craggy headlands
bleeding gold into the sea.

At the horizon's shimmering boundary
mainland Turkey snakes
bays and inlets wriggle menacingly
constant reminders of an old enmity.

Walking beautiful village streets
stones paved like patchwork quilts
bowers of bougainvillea bright against white houses.
In those tiny thoroughfares
blue front doors face each other like friends,
local residents smile
faces open and endearing.

And then, ascending wide well-worn steps
the colour of honey
up to the Holy Cave of the Apocalypse
where St John saw and heard
visions of a new world
archangels in flaming light
and folded wings
commanding the words
to flow into his mind.

The power of revelation
splitting the cave's roof in three
cleft apart
like a huge stone heart revealing its chambers
the blood of belief pulsing in the stone
the Orthodox priest sitting silently
in a chair by the wall, aware of its power.

By him at the window –
a scene of tumbling valleys
a racing hydrangea sea
protects the island like an apron
around a mother's waist.

I smelt the incense embedded
in the priest's long beard
and felt the holiness everywhere
likes flames against my skin
and all the air sucked out of me
as I trembled and softly wept.

And So They Wait for Love

For my sons

Both sons unfettered
but longing to be held
in love's embrace and gentle comforts.

Sometimes hopes and plans lay broken
then, a rally forwards
a desire to fit
like a foot into a shoe,
to walk life's journey with a beloved
from which all meaning flows.

I recognise in shadowed eyes
the heavy weight of aloneness
the stress of emptiness,
staring out at night upon the stars
all dimmed and closing in
like tiny fists
or like eyelids squeezed together.

Behind those lids
frightening bursts of colour
reduces them to small anxious boys.
What happens when the eyes are opened?

When did they realise
life's relentless demands
often thankless
are only softened
by sporadic snippets of sweetness?

One life is all there is.
This they have come to know.

And so they wait for love.

Sky Elephants

Sickle moon
Slices the sky
Like an ivory tusk

Clouds resemble elephants
Large, clumsy
Stampeding across heavens

Wind scatters the herd
Leaving wispy trails
Of scattered stardust

Sparrowsurge

Sparrowsurge!
A chirrup-chirp-chirp,
A downwards-darting,
Alighting on the grassy verge.

A chitter-chatter all-a-gather,
Frantic action,
Seeds a-swirling,
Staccato-rhythmed tiny beaks,
All dip-dip-dipping,
Heads a-turning, looking
Sweet sweet sweet.

Dappled feathers,
Windblown, ruffled
Eyes a-twinkling,
Fine legs dancing,
A flit-flit-flitting,
Pert-pretty-pert.
Sweet sprinkling of sparrowsurge!

Chapel Road

Sassafras, north-west Tasmania

Long sweep of gravel road
slips up and over the ridge.
Tiny wooden chapel
perched high
bereft in winter's cold grip.

Surrounded by green-quilted paddocks,
fat sheep and new-born lambs
it seems to say
'Where is my flock?'

Naked poplars stark,
ghostly-still.
A heavy sky presses down
upon seal-grey hills,
not a bird to be seen.

Black and white cows
heads bent,
munching their fill
resemble cardboard cut-outs
on a child's board game.

Restless fingers might pluck them up
re-arrange them at will
or obliterate the whole scene
with one sweep of an impatient hand.

Dawn Drifter

Winter dawn
Wakes in cold beauty,
Cold feather-light caress.

I feel her substance
Embrace her wonder
All her mystery felt within.

My inner voice cries out in joy
Speaking to the life without,
Let me hold you
Let me drift
And rise into your perfect light,
Into vast and airy realms
Not of this earth
Not you
Not I.

In reverence horizon melts
A slender band of rosy pearl.

For all the dawns that I have known
And all the dawns there are to come,
For all this living,
All this life,
Let praise be given.

Magnolias

(i)

As a candle's tallow
rich waxen petals of
ivory-rose flesh-flaming be

(ii)

A myriad of pink flamingos
feeding in the sun
resting on a leafy sea of green

Sunday Morning Rural Portrait

Claret ashes line the main street,
Bold against the blue-stained sky.
A long row of lovely redheads.

Laboured breath of Sunday morning joggers
Mists the air; feet crunching out a
Rhythm upon fallen leaves.

Last night a good rain fell,
The first steady soak of autumn.
Damp earth smells woody and sweet.

Cries of plover and gull entwine.
A haunting sound.
Somewhere a lone dog barks.

Distant hills are obscured by cloud.
The tallest peak breaks through the smokey vapours.
Reverent sky worshipper.

Wind, Roses and Wrens

Wind impatient
wakes me with its battering
windows rattled
unseen drumming fingers

White roses blown apart
fluttering whirling wheels
winged beings
scented dominions

thick stems of thorny canes
footholds for congregating wrens
sunshine-glossed eyes
tiny beaks in rapture

Birdsong tinkles
miniature bells within green temples
the listener, eyes closed
absorbs mantras of happiness

Tree Ship

The mighty trunk is a mast
Supporting massive limbs
Creaking and groaning
Like a wooden ship on water.
Leaves billow and flap,
Green sails singing.

It is a land-locked tree ship
Dreaming of an ocean
A stone's throw away.

Winter's Stage

Relentless rain
slices through the greyness.
Trees shake bunched fists
showering icy droplets.

Green sweep of foreshore park
a velvet cloth for springy footfalls,
All pervading dampness
cloys the air.

The sea hides behind a curtain,
clinging white mist.
It hangs like a stage prop,
plump, folded and secretive.

Starlings perch along power lines
flapping drenched wings,
They burst into song,
a chorus of drunken showgirls.

Armies of Light

To walk the earth
itself a living rock
is to sing to an existence
of many interwoven threads –
the fabric of creation's loom.

Automatic reflex sustains –
breathing of air
swallowing of water
food we eat –
Invisible these needs but needed,
one small part of a larger organism
that feeds us.

Even the tiny moth
beating paper-thin wings
upon the living air
has significance.

Some of our earth-bound days
are spent in slow movement and thought.
Melancholic and reflective,
people seem like wistful shadows
mingling with the angels.

In a quietness born of self
moments of awareness are pivotal,
teaching, bending, fusing,
translating words into deeds
and deeds into meaning.

One to another,
each to each other,
born as jewelled beings of pure beauty,
we are embraced by a knowing universe,
a living membrane rippling in its sac.

Humanity hums out its song
trembling within its own vibrations,
striving for the perfect note,
yet somewhere in the human intellect
a primal spirit hovers,
far removed from this millennium.

Passion-filled, reactionary
are those all-consuming thoughts
and the knowledge of their terrible wonder.
In that shadow
sleeps the genesis of greed and power,
good and evil.

We have learnt so much
yet understand little,
history repeated,
frightening consequences.
Can our next step be spiritual
no longer blinded by superficiality?

Upon the living rock
we are on a journey to the source,
as sunlight walks the sea
in vast armies of light.

Tell Me

Tell me
all is not lost.
Tell me
Each cell matters
before it shatters
absorbed
into star's dust.

All is delusion
an illusion,
hatred breeds fear
violence and division,
love in remission
human genius laid waste.

Enjoy the taste
of days unwinding,
the sun's rays
give us life
so we can live it.

Communicate.
Traverse heaven's gate,
spiral into highways
of purer thought.
Rediscover elation
in deeds of kindness
for all creation.

Here upon earth
in our gravity of being,
truth is in seeing
the beauty of our planet,
its wise blue eye
staring out at a cosmos
older than time.

Tell me
all is not lost
as the power
of a giant red sun
greets me each morning
with its rising.

North, south, east, west
wherever I turn
is the place that is best,
and when I lay my head
to rest
let it not be the end
but the beginning.

Acknowledgements

These poems were first published in the following books:

Emissaries of Light

'Behind the Screen', 'Gulls and Sky', 'Agapanthus in Moonlight', 'A Memory of Goolwa Beach', 'Blue-winged Angels', 'Transit of Venus – Alien Encounter', 'Death in Whyalla', 'Immigrants', 'Sparrowsurge', 'Dawn Drifter', 'Magnolias', 'Sunday Morning Rural Portrait', 'Winter's Stage' and 'Armies of Light'

Northern Lights

'Cameron Street Cameo', 'A Memory of Eastern European Migration', 'Four Candles For a Magyar', 'Welcome Home', 'Stone', 'Sea Horse', 'Helsinki', 'Lamentation on a Tribal Beach', 'The Ballad of Johnny', 'Patterns of Winter', 'Russell Square', 'Howard and Rudd Symphony', 'Wedge-tailed Eagle' and 'Tree Ship'

The Edge of Tranquillity

'Figures of Eight', 'Sky Elephants', 'Chapel Road' and 'Tell Me'

Handfuls of Promise

'Ferihegy Airport', 'Morning Walk', 'The Seventh Image', 'House of Dreams', 'Ice Age Oracle', 'News Item From Baghdad', 'Sanitised Terms of Warfare', 'Variations on Clouds', 'Walking and Watching', 'Acropolis at Night', 'Patmos', 'And So They Wait For Love' and 'Wind, Roses and Wrens'

Moonlight Wine (Pocket Poets)
'Choir Practice'

www.ingramcontent.com/pod-product-compliance
Lightning Source LLC
Chambersburg PA
CBHW062148100526
44589CB00014B/1735